Travis Gabler & Nicholas Nino

BUILD YOUR FINANCIAL BRIDGE

A Practical Guide to Building Lasting Financial Security

THE Short Book Formula PUBLISHING

Published by
The Short Book Formula Publishing

DISCLAIMER:
This book is intended for educational and informational purposes only. The content presented here represents the opinions and experiences of the author and should not be construed as specific financial, investment, tax, or legal advice. Every individual's financial situation is unique. Before making any financial decisions, readers should consult with qualified professionals who can evaluate their specific circumstances, needs, and goals. The examples, case studies, and scenarios presented in this book are for illustrative purposes only and do not guarantee or predict any particular outcome. Past performance is not indicative of future results. No reader should act or refrain from acting based solely on the information contained in this book without first seeking appropriate professional advice. The author, publisher, and any affiliated entities disclaim any liability for actions taken or not taken based on the contents of this book.

Contents

INTRODUCTION

The Golden Gate and Your Financial Future

IF YOU WANT TO get to your financial future, you need more than hope. You need a bridge.

You know that feeling when you look at your bank account and realize you're not where you thought you'd be? When you're making decent money but somehow still living paycheck to paycheck? When you're wondering if you'll ever be able to retire?

Yeah, I've been there. And so have most people navigating real financial pressure. You're not alone, and you're not behind. You just need a bridge. That's what this book is about. Not quick wins or overnight success stories but building something solid, something that lasts. A bridge between where you are today and where you want to go.

Let me tell you about one of the most impressive bridges I've ever seen because it's going to change how you think about your money.

The Bridge That Shouldn't Exist

The Golden Gate Bridge is one of those things you see, and it just stops you. It's bold, beautiful, and iconic. But it almost never happened.

Back in the early 1900s, engineers said it was im-possible. Too expensive, too dangerous. But one guy, Joseph Strauss, wouldn't let it go. He had the vision and his mantra was simple. "It *can* be done." And he kept showing up.

When World War I shut everything down. When the Great Depression killed the funding. When eleven workers died during construction. He kept showing up, and more than forty years after the first design sketches, the final bolt was finally in place.

→ Golden Gate Construction 1935

→ Golden Gate Bridge now (Picture taken 2017)

Now it's one of the most iconic structures in the world.

Forty years. Four decades of showing up, pushing through, never giving up. That's what it takes to create something that lasts.

How does this matter to your money? It might seem impossible right now, especially when you're dealing with competing priorities, unexpected expenses, and a world that keeps changing the rules. Maybe you're supporting kids while worrying about aging parents. Maybe you're trying to save for retirement while paying off a mortgage. Maybe you're just trying to figure out how to help your adult children without completely screwing over your own financial security.

Real life is messy. You're juggling multiple financial priorities, and most advice treats them like separate problems. They're not. They're all part of building one strong financial bridge that can handle whatever life throws at you.

And that's exactly why the get-rich-quick fantasy is so dangerous. When you're juggling real-life complexity, you need something solid, not a house of cards.

Building wealth isn't flashy. It's not quick. But it's absolutely doable. Even if you're starting later than you planned, you've made financial mistakes, or life keeps throwing curveballs. With the right vision and the discipline to keep building, you can create something that lasts.

It sounds easy, so why do so few people do it? Because nobody likes to hear that real results take real time.

The Fastest Way to Stay Broke

You've seen the promises, right? The Instagram ads. The friend who swears they're making a killing in crypto or day trading. And for just a moment, you wonder if maybe you should try it, too.

This has played out the same way for twenty years. Same story, different "shortcut." Trying to get rich quick is the fastest way to stay broke. The math is simple. Thirty years of steady, boring saving and investing has historically produced far more consistent outcomes than market timing — though no strategy guarantees specific results. Try to time the market or chase hot stocks? You're playing a game where the house always wins.

I know waiting isn't exciting. Nobody brags about their index funds at parties. But the alternative of jumping from one hot tip to the next, always chasing, never building, is a recipe for working until you're seventy.

The people who are thriving financially today didn't get there through a secret strategy. They built bridges strong enough to handle storms. Not overnight but through consistent action over time.

That's the kind of foundation you need. One built for the reality of life that assumes chaos instead of calm.

You don't build the Golden Gate Bridge in six months. And you don't build financial security by chasing perfect timing. You build it one decision at a time, one month at a time. A plan designed to hold strong through whatever comes next.

Will it take longer than you want? Yeah, probably. Is it worth it? Absolutely.

So how do you build this thing? How do you go from wanting financial security to having it?

The Three Things Every Financial Bridge Needs

To make your bridge as sturdy as possible, it comes down to three critical parts. Miss one and it won't hold when life gets complicated.

First thing - Vision: You've got to know where you're going. What does financial success look like for you? Is it being able to care for aging parents without going broke? Retiring to a beach town where you spend most of your time painting? Taking your grandkids on an epic trip every year? Get specific. Write it down.

Make it real. When life gets complicated, and it will, your vision is what keeps you on track.

Second - Reality: Get honest about your numbers. What's your real financial picture? How much debt do you have? What are you really spending each month? Are your current financial habits sustainable? The numbers don't lie, but they don't judge you, either.

Third - Action: You've got to do the real work of building your bridge. This is where you have to keep saving for retirement while your kid needs help with student loans. Where you might choose to bring coffee from home instead of buying it every day. This is where you learn that building wealth isn't in one perfect decision but taking small actions consistently over time, even when life is messy and complicated.

Once you know where you want to go and where you are, then comes the part that separates the dreamers from the builders...doing the work.

Setbacks to your plan are inevitable. Markets will crash. Jobs will be lost. Parents will need care. Kids will need help. But when you're crystal clear on your vision and you have a plan built to handle these realities, you don't just survive the storms.

You come out stronger, just like the Golden Gate Bridge.

The builders didn't hope for perfect conditions; they planned for earthquakes, wind, and decades of heavy traffic. They built something that could handle it all and stand the test of time. That's exactly what we're going to do for you.

Your Personal Golden Gate Bridge

10Every chapter in this book is designed to help you build one piece of your financial bridge. By the end, you'll have more than just a blueprint for your future. You'll have a real-world plan that connects your money to what matters in your values, priorities, and the life you want.

Financial security isn't just numbers. It's freedom. It's creating options. It's making sure the life you're working so hard for is the one you get to live.

That doesn't happen overnight. But it does happen if you're willing to be patient, strategic, and consistent. It doesn't matter whether you're starting at twenty-five for fifty-five. What matters is that you start.

You can keep doing what you're doing and hope things magically improve, or you can build something solid that gets you where you want to go.

Your call.

CHAPTER 1

Start at Your Finish Line - Visualizing Your Bridge

WHEN YOU WERE A kid, maybe you dreamed of being an astronaut or a basketball player. You'd lie in bed visualizing what life could look like. The whole world felt possible.

Then you got older. Marriage, kids, mortgage, and a career. Now you just think about surviving the day, paying the bills, and keeping everyone fed. That childlike daydreaming? It disappears.

You're making good money and know you should save more. But visualizing retirement? Letting yourself dream? It feels unrealistic.

But the thing is, bringing back that childlike energy is where the best financial conversations begin. I know it sounds corny, but stick with me. This approach has completely transformed how people think about money.

Many high-income professionals are doing the basics, contributing to a 401(k), but beyond that? Life is too busy to think much further ahead.

What surprises them? They've never asked the real questions about what they want their money to do. Do we want to buy a vacation home? Retire to Hawaii? Send our grandkids to college? What do we want to do with this money we've been earning?

Most couples avoid that conversation. It's too abstract. They have no urgency and no time for dreaming when you're drowning in today. But when couples finally have this conversation, the best approach isn't to start with the numbers. Start by dreaming together. What does your ideal retirement look like? Where are you? What are you doing?

Once that vision gets clear, *then* we run the numbers. Vague goals like "retire someday" don't inspire action, but the image of a beach house with a dream kitchen, summers in Italy with grandkids, or helping your kids buy their first home? That gets people moving.

Now they're not just saving for retirement. They're building toward a future they can see and feel. And that makes all the difference.

Vague goals don't inspire. You need something compelling. You need a vision so specific that when you're tempted to spend on something that doesn't matter, you can picture that dream. The ocean breeze, the Aperol spritz in the piazza and think, "Actually, I'd rather have that."

That's why we start at your finish line.

Why Your Dreams Matter More Than Your Budget

Once that vision is clear, the real magic begins.

The truth is most people don't have a money problem. They have a clarity problem. Without a clear destination, every financial choice becomes disconnected. You grab the $6 Starbucks every day instead of brewing at home and putting that money toward the house you've always wanted. You book a last-minute trip instead of building your emergency fund. Every choice becomes disconnected from the bigger picture.

But when people reconnect with those bigger dreams and *then* show them the numbers, something clicks. Those "impossible" goals? Half the time, they're totally doable. We just need to build the bridge.

The work is matching those goals to the numbers. That's way more motivating than "save for retirement."

Once you know the destination, we build the bridge.

Studies show you're twice as likely to achieve goals when you write them down and review them often. Makes sense, right? When it's top of mind, you make different choices. You pause before you spend. You remember why you're making sacrifices.

Having someone hold you accountable to your vision, not just the numbers, makes a real difference. Even when life gets messy. Because at the end of the day, you can do this.

The catch is, it's hard to stay accountable to a vision you've never talked about, especially with the person you're building your life with.

That's why the next step is so important.

The Conversation Every Couple Needs to Have

Most couples have never talked about money beyond logistics. They know who pays which bills, but they've never dreamed together about what comes next.

I get it. Between kids, careers, and everyday chaos, it feels like something you'll get to later. But you don't want to wake up one day and realize you're heading toward completely different futures, or worse, no vision at all.

I tell couples to get out of the house. Go to the beach. Take a walk. Book a night away. Find space to talk without distractions. Then ask the real questions. What do we want our life to look like? What does retirement mean to us? Where are we? What are we doing?

At first, most couples fumble through it. One person talks about travel. The other mentions staying close to the grandkids. Sometimes they realize they've never said these dreams out loud, not even to themselves.

But then something changes. They listen. They laugh. They discover unexpected alignment, or at least a starting point to build from. And suddenly, the future feels real.

Once that vision is shared, every financial decision becomes easier. Now you're building something together.

Vague Dreams vs. Specific Visions

People stay stuck when their goals are too vague to act on. They sound more like hopes than plans:

"I want to retire someday."

"It would be nice to send the kids to college."

"We should probably buy a house eventually."

These aren't goals. They're hopes without deadlines.

Here's what clarity actually sounds like:

"I want to retire at sixty-seven, in thirteen years. We'll downsize to a smaller house near the beach... something with a great kitchen, so I can get back into cooking. I want to take one amazing family vacation every year and be the grandparent who flies the whole family to Italy."

Feel the difference? That's not just a goal. That's a vision you can see. You can smell the ocean breeze. You can see your grandkids staring up at the Colosseum.

When you get that specific, you're not making sacrifices; you're making investments in a future that you're excited about.

The "Uh Oh" Moment

Even with the best intentions, some people still need a wake-up call. It's usually a life event, like a death, a health scare, or a layoff. Suddenly, they realize they've been on autopilot and start asking, "Where do we really stand?"

That's when we run the numbers. And sometimes, I have to deliver tough news.

"Based on what you've saved and how you're spending, you've got a 40 percent chance of retiring at sixty-five with the lifestyle you want."

I call this the *uh oh* moment.

It's tough but necessary.

The moment of clarity, especially when it's painful, is what finally gets people serious about their goals.

One man came in after his best friend had a heart attack at fifty-eight. It rattled him. They were the same age, living similar lives, and it made him realize he'd never stopped to check where he stood.

That moment got him through the door.

Until then, he made great money, but he never looked at the numbers. When we finally ran them, the picture wasn't great. Retiring at sixty-five was unlikely. Maybe not even sixty-seven. But instead of shutting down, he got serious. For the first time, he wrote down what he really wanted. Then we reverse-engineered a plan to get there.

Two years later, he's on track. Same income. Same life. But now he knows exactly where he's headed.

That's the power of building your bridge to a future you can really see.

Making Dreams Feel Real (Not Like Homework)

Let's be honest, nobody gets excited about SMART goals. The whole thing feels like corporate homework. Eyes glaze over.

What really works? Conversations and stories.

Stories of people living their dreams are everywhere. The retiree who splits the year between France and the States. The single mom who saved up and bought her first house. The couple who takes their extended family on a dream vacation every year.

Seeing stories like these is exciting. They see people just like them living incredible lives and realize this is possible.

That excitement is fuel. At the start of your bridge, you're pumped, like joining a gym in January. But over time, people lose steam. Life gets busy. Immediate wants feel more urgent than long-term goals.

That's human nature.

This is why writing down your vision matters. Even more powerful is having someone remind you of it regularly. Regular check-ins with someone who knows your vision can bring you back on track. 'Didn't you say owning your own place was the priority? Here's how we stay on track.'"

The right vision refocuses people fast. It turns every financial choice into a step toward the life you want. When couples align on that vision, everything moves in the same direction.

Your Dreams Are the Bridge

Financial planning isn't about restriction or guilt. It's about building a bridge from where you are to where you're going. But you can't build it until you know what's on the other side.

Get specific. Write it down. Share it with someone who'll keep you accountable. And when life gets busy and your dreams start feeling distant, come back to this chapter.

Your dreams aren't too big. They're more doable than you think. We just need the plan.

Now that you know where you're going, let's get honest about where you are.

CHAPTER 2

Know Your Starting Point - Honest Financial Assessment

YOU'VE DONE THE FUN part in visualizing your dreams, picturing your retirement, and getting excited about what's possible. You know what's waiting on the other side of your bridge.

Now let's talk about where you're starting from. I mean an honest financial assessment, not what you think or feel, but what the numbers truly say.

This is where most people want to change the subject. They'd rather put their head in the sand than look at assets, liabilities, and cash flow. But you can't build a bridge if you don't know your starting point. And that starts with looking in the mirror.

I get it. You want to skip straight to investing and compound interest. But none of that matters until you look at the numbers.

You Can't Fake the Numbers

The numbers don't lie. They either work or they don't. Once you have that future vision,the work is matching your finances to your goals.

It's time to be *proactive* instead of *reactive*.

When someone wants to retire but their assets and income don't add up, that's not bad news. It's clarity. Now we know where you're starting from and can course correct. We don't have to fix everything overnight. But we do want to look for small changes that will compound over time.

If the numbers show you're on track? Even better. Now we can enhance the situation. The key is honesty, clarity, and the choice to make better decisions aligned with your vision. Knowing your numbers is empowering.

Your Real Financial Picture Might Surprise You

Most people have never taken a real look at their finances. They pay bills and save a little, but the complete picture? They're flying blind. After years of studying financial behavior, a pattern emerges. When we run the real numbers, people have either a pleasant surprise or wake-up call.

The Pleasant Surprise

Some clients are terrified to retire, even after decades of disciplined planning. I'm talking about the super-savers who've lived frugally, steadily built wealth but still struggle to enjoy it.

Consider someone who spent forty years in pharmacy. Never married, no kids. She'd saved and saved for decades. When she finally ran her numbers, she had more than enough to last well beyond her nineties. But the idea of spending $15,000 on a vacation? She couldn't bring herself to even consider it.

Then things got real. In her sixties, facing a health issue that made time feel limited, she finally admitted she dreamed of taking fifteen family members to the Galapagos Islands.

That's when I asked her the hard question:

"Do you want to give with warm hands or cold hands? We could pull $100,000 from your portfolio right now, and you wouldn't even feel it. But this trip? It will create memories that last beyond your lifetime."

With that perspective in the back of her mind, she finally took the trip. It became a once-in-a-lifetime experience her family will never forget.

The lesson from stories like hers is that money is just a tool. The goal is finding the balance between planning for tomorrow and enjoying today. What's the saving for if you never let yourself use it?

The Wake-Up Call

The Pleasant Surprise happens, but more clients fall into The Wake-Up Call category. These are people making great money who assume they're crushing it financially.

But once we run the numbers, a different story emerges. They are big spenders with big lifestyles and little to show for it. I live in Los Angeles where that's the norm. We're surrounded by great restaurants, beaches, and endless things to do. It's incredibly easy to spend your entire income without even realizing it.

Consider an attorney with a big income, luxury car, expensive restaurants. He looked like a million bucks (and was earning it, too). But when we ran his numbers? He had $50,000 in credit card debt.

He had the cash to wipe it out. The problem was, he wasn't paying attention. Everything was on autopay, so the debt just sat there, quietly accruing 10 percent interest (non-deductible, by the way). When I pointed that out, he was embarrassed.

Being faced with the numbers was his wake-up call.

The great news? In one year, his retirement projections went from less than a 20 percent probability to over 95 percent[1], just by cutting expenses and adding a savings plan. And he was still able to enjoy his life. Sushi dinners three nights a week instead of seven. Not picking up the check for the entire group every time. Small changes that let him keep his lifestyle while securing his future.

The goal is finding that balance: not too much spending, not too much saving with no life.

The 50/20/30 System: Your Financial Foundation

The 50/20/30 rule is a budget system recommended by the Certified Financial Planner® Board (CFP®). But don't let that formal name scare you. It's very simple.

1 This scenario is for illustrative purposes only; results vary based on individual circumstances

Take your total income, and split it three ways. Half goes to the expenses you can't avoid, a fifth goes to building your future, and the rest is yours to enjoy.

That's it. The beauty of this system is that you're not choosing between saving for retirement or enjoying life. You're doing both.

WHAT YOUR 50/20/30 LOOKS LIKE

50 percent - Must-Have Expenses The unavoidable stuff: mortgage, rent, utilities, groceries, transportation (car payment, gas, insurance), health insurance, minimum debt payments. Spending more than 50 percent here? Time to trim.

20 percent - Financial Goals Building your future: 401(k), IRA, Roth accounts, emergency fund, paying down debt faster than required, college savings, brokerage investments. Anything that improves your net worth goes here.

30 percent - Lifestyle and Discretionary The fun stuff: restaurants, entertainment, travel, hobbies, gym memberships. This is where you enjoy your money.

We've got tools to help you map this out. But right now, just take action. Grab a napkin if that's what gets you started. What matters is tracking where your money goes.

If you're not hitting your 20 percent savings goal, we'll evaluate. Do you *really* need Nobu three times a week, or could once a month work?

When someone has an aggressive goal like buying a house in an expensive market, the move is to shift 10 percent from lifestyle to put 30 percent toward goals instead of 20 percent.

When someone is dead serious about a goal, they'll hit it much faster than someone who makes more money but doesn't take it seriously. It's not about how much you make but how focused you are on what you want.

Automation makes this even easier. I've got three kids, I'm married, and life is full, so I'm a big fan of automation. Set up auto-deposits into savings and investment accounts. Out of sight, out of mind. Once it becomes a habit, our goal is to increase it each year. Small changes now compound into big results later.

But even with the perfect system and all the automation in the world, none of it matters if you're still telling yourself the same old stories.

The Mirror Moment: Two Lies That Keep You Stuck

The numbers don't lie. But most people avoid looking at them. Two lies come up again and again that keep people stuck.

The "Later" Lie: "I'll get my finances in order *after* I get married/buy a house/have kids/get that promotion." The problem is that "later" keeps moving. People snap their fingers and realize five years have passed with no progress.

The "I'm Fine" Lie: "I make good money, so I must be in great shape." But when we run the numbers, the reality is very different. Sometimes better than expected, sometimes much worse.

Both lies serve the same purpose in that they let you avoid looking in the mirror.

When clients get honest about their numbers, they sometimes feel guilt or shame. Don't. Knowing exactly where you stand is the fastest way to get where you want to go. The most empowering thing you can do is be brutally honest. Are you overspending? Do the numbers match what you think? Are you using "someday" to avoid taking action?

Your future self will thank you for having the courage to face reality now. Once you know your true starting point, we can tackle dealing with debt and building wealth habits, the two things that make or break your financial bridge.

CHAPTER 3

Dealing with Debt and Building Wealth Habits

YOU'VE TAKEN THE HARDEST step by looking at your numbers. You know your vision and your starting point. Now we start to build the bridge to get there.

First up? A clear picture of your debt. Take it from someone who's made all the mistakes. When I started this career at twenty-one, I was the poster child for what *not* to do. As I gave advice on saving for the future, I was spending my own money on trips to Vegas and dinners I couldn't afford. I felt invincible. I thought I'd always have a job and could always make more money.

My wake-up call came during the 2008 financial crisis. My pay got cut just as I was getting engaged, and suddenly I couldn't out-earn my spending anymore. That's when I learned that not all debt is created equally.

This changes how to think about every dollar of debt. Some debt can destroy your bridge before you even start building it, while other debt can, surprisingly, help you build wealth.

Good Debt vs. Bad Debt: It's Simple

Understanding the difference between good and bad debt can save you thousands of dollars and years of stress.

Good debt is debt interest you can deduct on your taxes, like mortgage interest and student loan interest. Deductible doesn't mean "free." You can absolutely over leverage yourself with too much mortgage debt, and whether you can take the deduction depends on your income and tax situation.

A 4 percent mortgage becomes 3 percent after tax deductions. That's the kind of debt that works for you, not against you.

Bad debt is everything else, such as credit cards, car loans, and personal loans. This debt is non-deductible. Every dollar of interest you pay comes straight out of your pocket with zero tax benefit. And the interest rates? Usually way higher. We're talking 18 to 25 percent on credit cards and 6 to 8 percent on car loans.

Bad debt actively works against you every day.

Imagine a couple — the husband an economist, a smart guy with a successful career, but they had

$40,000 in credit card debt spread across Nordstrom and Neiman Marcus cards. The interest rates were upwards of 20 to 25 percent.

They had the money to pay it all off. But they'd gotten comfortable with the lifestyle, and the debt just kept accumulating. They were in their late thirties and wanted to retire early.

When I showed them the numbers, they got serious. They completely changed their lifestyle. No more shopping sprees, no more keeping up with appearances. They got aggressive about eliminating that bad debt.

Fast forward ten years, and they're multi-millionaires with zero consumer debt. They're on track to retire[2] at fifty-three, not sixty-five. Now they're using good debt strategically, borrowing against their portfolio to buy rental properties. They went from drowning in bad debt to leveraging good debt to build even more wealth.

That's the power of understanding the difference and taking action. But understanding it doesn't help if you won't look at it.

They weren't special. They just faced reality. Here's

2 This scenario is for illustrative purposes only; results vary based on individual circumstances.

how you do the same.

Face Your Debt Head-On

Most people bury their head in the sand with debt. They make minimum payments, avoid statements, and hope it'll get better on its own. But facing your debt head-on is a relief.

When someone gets proactive about their debt, a clear strategy makes a real difference. A debt calculator can show the exact date the last payment will be made. Seeing that end date gives real motivation to stay on track.

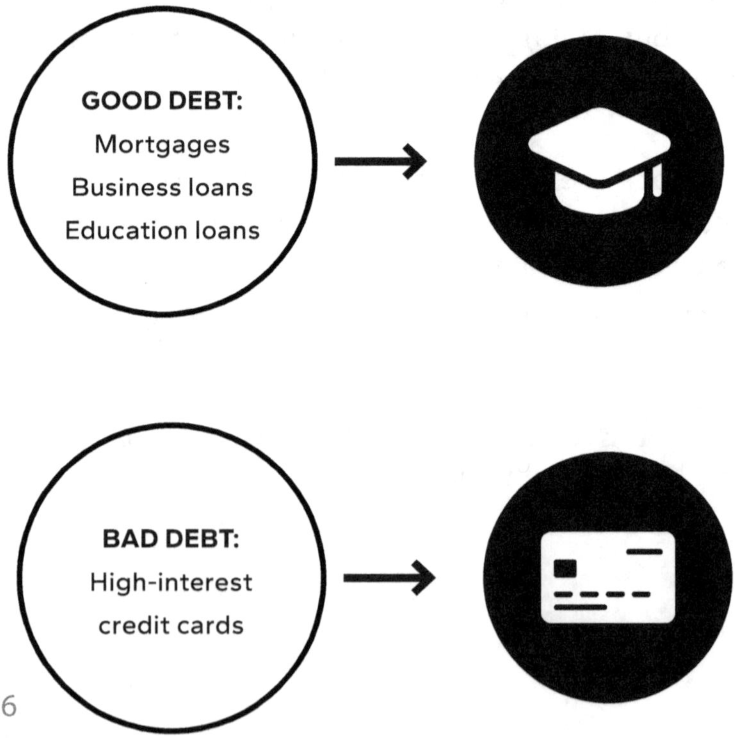

Even while paying off debt, you can still allocate funds toward your goals and lifestyle using that 50/20/30 framework. Twenty percent still goes toward goals (which now includes debt elimination), and thirty percent stays for lifestyle expenses.

Over time, you build the habits to stay consistent with payments, then start paying off more than required, until you're completely debt free. It takes discipline but beats hoping for the best.

That strategy matters because there's a daily force that's either building your wealth or destroying it. Let me show you what I mean.

Why Compound Interest Can Make or Break You

Compound interest doesn't care about your intentions. It's going to compound whether you're building wealth or drowning in debt.

When you're carrying credit card debt at 20 percent interest, that interest is compounding against you daily. You think you're making progress with payments, but the interest keeps building on itself. It's brutal.

Flip that around. When compound interest works *for* you through savings and investments, it's like having money that makes money while you sleep.

Investing is easy now. You can buy into thousands of stocks with a few clicks. The hard part is saving money. It takes real discipline to set aside money today for some future version of yourself.

To build the habit, start small. Increase every year. There's real power in knowing you saved more this year than last year. That's where compound interest becomes your best friend. Time and consistency turn small amounts into something significant.

So how do you harness this power without overwhelm? How do you build these habits when life is already crazy? Most people try to fix everything at once and fail. But there's a better way.

The 1 Percent Better Philosophy

Whether tackling debt or building savings, the philosophy is to simply get 1 percent better. That's it.

Save 5 percent this year. Next year make it 6 percent. Year after, 7 percent.

Doesn't sound life-changing, right? But when December rolls around, you're not beating yourself up about money anymore. You saved more than last year. You can see the progress. That's when building wealth stops feeling impossible and starts feeling inevitable.

The most financially successful people aren't the highest earners; they're the most disciplined savers who applied this 1 percent philosophy year after year. They live within their means, save consistently, and do it for decades. Consider a couple, both teachers, who started at 5 percent savings in their thirties. Every year, they bumped it up 1 percent. By retirement, they were saving 25 percent without feeling it because they built up to it gradually.

It's your habits, not your income.

Small Daily Habits That Make the Biggest Long-Term Difference

When you're clear on your goal, like buying your first home, suddenly bringing lunch to work instead of buying it doesn't feel like sacrifice. It feels like progress.

Twenty bucks a day on lunch? That's $5,000 a year. Invested over 20 years, you're looking at $30,000... from brown-bagging it[3].

I know it isn't exciting. Nobody's posting on Instagram about bumping their 401(k) contribution from 3 to 4 percent. But when it comes to your financial bridge, boring works. The people who embrace 'get rich slow' are the ones who actually get rich.

3 Hypothetical example; assumes consistent investment returns.

Get Rich Slow: The Strategy That Works

If you want the lowest possible chance of financial success, try to get rich quick. If you want what works, get rich slow.

Boring money never goes to zero. The people who build wealth create discipline over decades, add small increases every year, and stay the course no matter what. When you stick to proven strategies, you're not gambling with your future. You're building it.

Nobody ever says, "I wish I saved less money." They understand that building their financial bridge isn't in perfection but persistence. Small, consistent actions win.

Now I know you're thinking, *"If I have to get rich slow, aren't I already behind?"* Yeah, the best time to start would've been ten years ago. But the next best time? Right now.

You've got your debt strategy down. You understand how compound interest works. You're building the habits one percent at a time. Most people blow it all up when they let their emotions take over when it's time to invest.

Next, I'm going to show you why boring investing beats exciting investing every single time and how to stay calm when everyone else is losing their minds.

CHAPTER 4

Investing Without the Emotional Rollercoaster

IN 2008, DURING THE height of the behavioral finance research surge, everything the textbooks were teaching. Suddenly everything I was learning in textbooks was happening in real time with actual people sitting across from my desk.

Picture person after person sharing the same gut-wrenching story. “Travis, Nick, I lost my job. I’m down 30 percent in my portfolio. They’re foreclosing on my house.” At the time, it was the second worst financial disaster in U.S. history besides the Great Depression. No pressure, right?

Looking back, being green probably saved me. If something as massive as the collapse of Lehman

Brothers happened now, it would shake me to my core. But back then, I had that invincible twenty-something mentality that let me do the most important thing.

Show up.

For each person I had to tell them they couldn't retire because they were suddenly down 25 percent, I learned I didn't need to have all the answers; I just needed to show up. While a lot of advisors went quiet during the crisis, the ones who showed up made the difference.

No matter what's happening in the moment, staying focused on the long term is what matters. Let me share the three concepts that keep you grounded when everyone else is losing their minds.

The Three Money Concepts That Actually Matter

These concepts separate wealth chasers from wealth builders:

Time Value of Money: Why the Rich Actually Get Richer

Money today is worth more than money tomorrow because it can start working immediately. It's like planting a tree. The earlier you plant, the sooner you get shade.

The wealthy understand this. They get their money working early and let time do the heavy lifting. The earlier you start, the more time your money has to multiply.

Compound Interest: Einstein's Favorite Discovery

Einstein called compound interest the eighth wonder of the world. "He who understands it, earns it; he who doesn't, pays it."

You're not just earning returns on what you invested. You're earning returns on your returns. Like a snowball rolling downhill, it becomes an avalanche.

Dollar Cost Averaging: Your Emotional Insurance Policy

Dollar cost averaging means you invest the same dollar amount, every month, like clockwork. When the market is expensive, you buy fewer shares. When it's cheap, you buy more.

Instead of buying when everyone's excited or panic-selling when things tank, this strategy forces you to be smart even when emotions are high.

Once you get these three concepts working together, you've created an unstoppable wealth-building machine.

Now, you might be thinking, *"Great concepts, but what happens when I'm watching my account drop 30 percent?"* Fair question. Let me show you what's at stake when you let emotion override logic, even when you know better.

When Smart People Make Terrible Money Decisions

There's real science behind why fear or excitement leads brilliant people to make awful investment choices. My Behavioral Finance Designation taught me the concepts, but two decades of client work showed me how it plays out.

The Vegas analogy nails it. When you're up, you want to keep playing. When you're down, you either panic or double down. Both impulses are wrong.

The market triggers the same emotions. Up markets make you feel invincible; down markets make you feel doomed. Neither reflects reality. The key is seeing past the feelings to the numbers that matter and the discipline to stick to the plan.

INVESTING AND THE "EMOTIONAL ROLLERCOASTER"

When the markets test your confidence
in your investing strategy

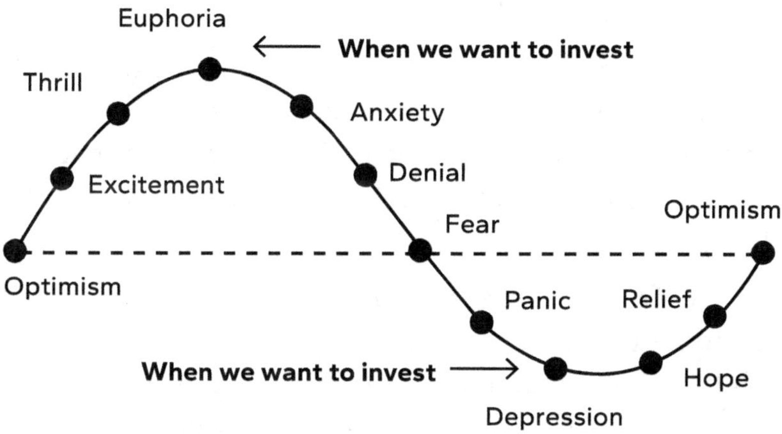

FEELING THE UPS AND DOWNS:

During periods of market volatility it's easy to let emotions take over and lose sight of your long-term goals. Investors may feel more confident about taking action when the markets are going up, but the best opportunities are available when investors feel the worst.

When Discipline Beats Panic

Today I've lived through five market downturns of 20 percent or more. In all five situations, clients who stayed the course by staying invested made it back to all-time highs.[4]

The 2008 financial crisis and the 2020 COVID crash are two moments that stand out to me.

The financial crisis was a deep economic wound affecting everything, including real estate, stocks, bonds, and businesses. It took about five years to get back to even. Clients who stayed invested were rewarded slowly, year after year.

The COVID crisis was unprecedented. The market plummeted, then rebounded months later to all-time highs. People who panic-sold missed the steepest recovery in history. Those who showed patience were rewarded quickly.

That doesn't mean they didn't feel fear. They absolutely did. The difference is not letting feelings dictate decisions. Instead, we let numbers like historical metrics and return averages guide the path forward. Time *in* the market, not *timing* the market. The more boring it feels, the better the results tend to be.

4 Past performance does not guarantee future results.

Why Boring Always Wins

Boring money is the best kind of money

My dad taught me this lesson without realizing it. He was a junior high math teacher who never changed schools or chased the next big thing. He just consistently contributed to his teacher's pension, got the district match, and let compound growth do its work.

That pension was a forced savings plan that removed emotion. Every paycheck, money went in. Through recessions and boom times, it didn't matter. The contributions kept going, and he never had to make fear-based decisions.

By retirement, that boring, consistent approach set him up completely. No market timing. No hot stock chasing. Just time in the market. While others jumped jobs, potentially losing pension benefits, my dad stayed the course, and it paid off.

Boring doesn't make headlines. It doesn't impress at parties. But boring retires comfortably while exciting is still working at seventy.

How "Exciting" Investments Become Expensive Lessons

During the real estate boom, a successful small business owner decided to go all in. Like most entrepreneurs, he preferred tangible assets to intangible ones. He loved things he could see and touch.

He'd heard Utah real estate was the place to double your money and earn passive income. He lived in Southern California but bought four homes in Utah, sight unseen.

Entrepreneurs bet on themselves. It works for their business, but the same risk appetite can destroy them in the markets. When the crash hit, those four Utah properties turned into financial quicksand. Within a year and a half, he'd foreclosed on all of them.

The ripple effects hit his whole family with no more vacations or business expansions. Just survival mode.

When markets are up, your brain tricks you into thinking the streak will last forever.

My favorite warning sign is when my mom starts asking me about it. She's amazing, but when your hairdresser, neighbor, or mom starts talking about an investment, smart money has already moved on. That's your cue to pause.

I'm not opposed to exciting investments. But maybe 3 to 5 percent of your assets go there. The rest? The boring, proven stuff.

You only need to get rich once. And there are only two paths to get there, either the flashy, high-risk way that rarely works, or the slow, methodical way that does. I'll take the boring path every time.

The Window Pane Theory of Risk

No matter what path you choose, diversification protects you from emotional mistakes.

Imagine you have one giant window. A baseball smashes through it, and you have to replace the whole thing. But if you have ten panes and one breaks, you replace just that one.

That's exactly how diversification works in your portfolio. If one stock or investment tanks, diversification means only one out of ten holdings gets hurt, while the other nine might go up.

Diversification protects you from big losses, but it also means you won't hit every home run. You don't have to swing for the fences every time, but stay in the game long enough for compound growth to work in your favor.

EMBRACE ASSET ALLOCATION

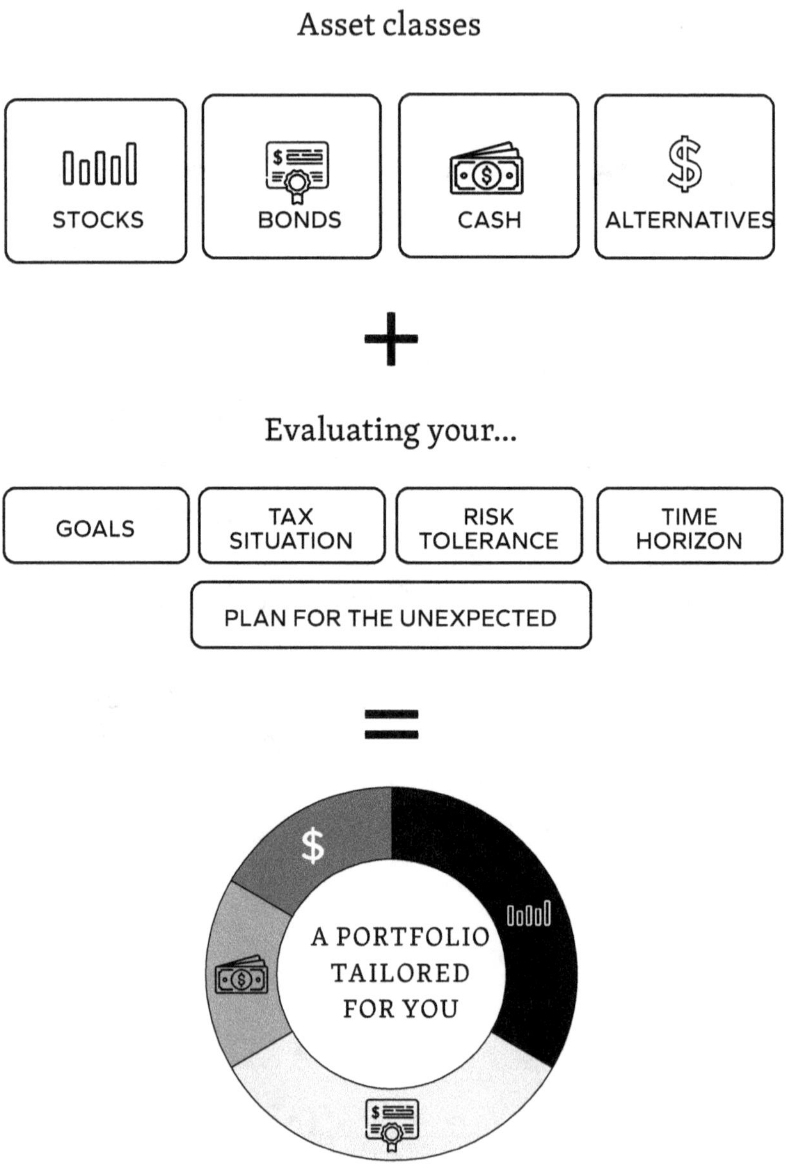

EMBRACE DIVERSIFICATION AND ASSET ALLOCATION

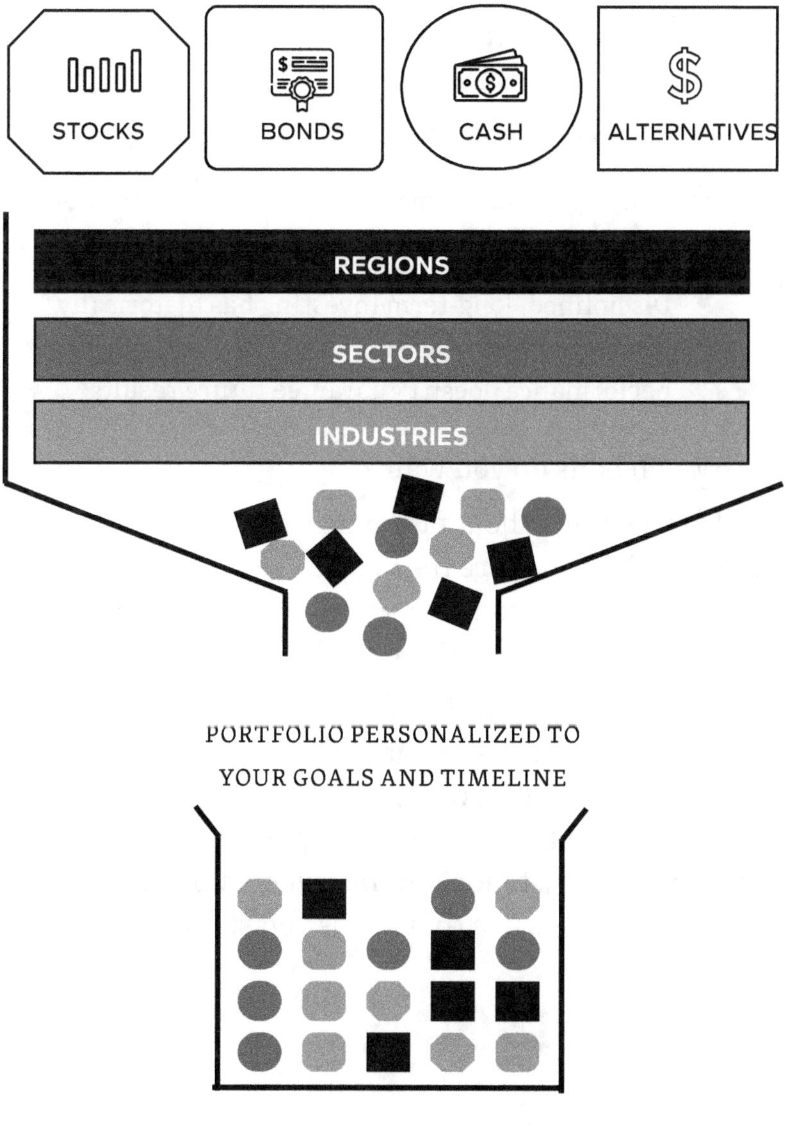

The Investment Truth

Social media turned everyone into day traders. Your cousin made a killing on crypto. Your coworker doubled their money on some Reddit stock.

What they don't post are people who lost everything chasing the same dream.

The reality is straightforward:

- Chasing hot investments rarely delivers the outcomes people hope for
- Disciplined, long-term investing has historically produced more consistent outcomes — though past performance doesn't guarantee future results

Which odds do you want?

No one brags about bumping their 401(k) from 3 to 4 percent. But those are the people I see retiring comfortably. That boring consistency separates wealth builders from wealth chasers. Get rich slow!

Remember, we're building your financial bridge. Every boring investment decision is another steel beam. Every consistent contribution is another support cable. The exciting stuff? That's paint and decorations. They are pretty to look at, but when storms come, it's the boring structure that keeps you standing.

CHAPTER 5

Planning for a Confident Retirement

TWO THINGS ARE CERTAIN. Someday you'll stop working, and someday you'll die.

I know, not exactly cocktail party conversation. But the people who acknowledge these certainties live far better lives than the ones who stick their heads in the sand.

The Hollywood Hills Reality Check

Consider an attorney making half a million a year. A beautiful house in the Hollywood Hills, fancy cars, living the dream. But when we ran his retirement numbers, it was a brutal wake-up call.

Based on his saving versus spending[5], he had a 50 percent probability of successful retirement at sixty-five. Fifty percent. A coin flip.

It's hard to deliver that message to someone who's so outwardly successful. "What do you mean 50 percent? I make half a million dollars!"

What makes this process powerful is that numbers don't lie. There's nothing subjective about the math. Here are your assets, liabilities and expenses, and they don't add up to the retirement plan you want. There's no way around it.

Once we acknowledged the facts, there was good news. He had plenty of time to make changes and get on track.

We started with a savings goal of 10 percent gross income with an increase over time. Through small systematic changes over a few years, he moved his retirement probability from 50 percent to over 90 percent. Nothing dramatic was required, just consistent, incremental progress.

That attorney's transformation illustrates something crucial. Retirement planning isn't about deprivation or some far-off fantasy. Rather, it means building something so solid that work becomes optional, not mandatory.

---

5 For illustrative purposes only; results vary based on individual circumstances.

The Most Important Bridge: From Working to Retired

The biggest financial bridge we build is from "working" to "retired." And retired, for us, isn't about hitting sixty-five and collecting a gold watch. It's about having the ability to be 100 percent financially stable and never have to work again.

Retirement is the most rewarding bridge to cross. Nobody ever says, 'I wish I saved less money for retirement.

There's a psychological advantage to watching your savings grow year over year. Knowing you saved more this year than last year creates momentum. It reinforces that you're on track for the vision of life you want to create.

But before we dive into how to build this bridge, we need to talk about something nobody wants to discuss.

The Two Retirement Phases: Accumulation and Withdrawal

A successful retirement depends on the actions you take leading up to it. We plan your bridge to retirement based on accumulation and withdrawal, two separate phases.

The Accumulation Phase

When you're actively working, the goal is to accumulate enough money to retire based on your personal timeline. Using the CFP® Board standard, save 10 percent or more of your total income (and increase this amount over time). That's the baseline that works.[6]

The secret is "forced savings" to make it automatic before you ever see the money. Set up your contributions to flow into your main retirement vehicles like your 401(k), Roth IRA, or taxable brokerage.

The beautiful thing is that once you set up forced savings into these accounts, instead of guilt about another wasted year, you realize you saved $20,000 without even thinking about it! Your bridge gets stronger every year.

Most people stop here. They master saving but never learn the most important part: spending. Building wealth is only half the equation. The other half is turning it into income you can retire on.

The Withdrawal Phase

The real shift happens here.

You've spent decades getting a paycheck. Direct deposit hits, bills get paid, life moves forward. Then one day, that stops. No more W-2s. No more automatic

---

6 These are general guidelines. Consult a financial professional for advice specific to your situation.

deposits. No more taxes being quietly withheld behind the scenes.

Now you become your own payroll department. So how do you give yourself a paycheck now that you don't have one coming in?

A simple rule of thumb is to plan on withdrawing 4 to 5 percent of your portfolio every year. This creates a sustainable paycheck that accounts for market volatility and the reality that you might live to ninety-five. Some years you'll pull less when markets tank; some years maybe a bit more when they're flying. The key is having a system that won't leave you broke at eighty-five.

What separates people who just retire from those who retire well? They don't pull money randomly. They position money strategically to minimize taxes and keep more of it.

PROTECTION PLANNING: THE BRIDGE TO THE UNKNOWN

You can build the perfect retirement bridge, but life doesn't always go according to plan. Protection is about ensuring unexpected events don't destroy what you've built.

What Happens When Life Throws You a Curve ball

One of my earliest clients taught me this the hard way. A blue-collar guy who worked at a meatpacking plant for thirty-five years, very salt of the earth. When he retired, he confided he hadn't been a great dad, but he planned to spend the rest of his life making it right with his kids and grandkids. →

And for a while, he did. I'd stop by his house for stories about family BBQs and birthday parties. He'd send me home with avocados from his backyard trees.

Then came the heart attack. Suddenly, he was gone.

He'd saved perfectly for retirement. There was life insurance, so his family was okay financially. There was no forced sale of the house, and his grandkids' college funds were intact. But his time was cut short. The years he'd planned to repair relationships were over. That's the one thing insurance couldn't replace.

That's what protection planning is *really* about. Without it, even worse things happen. The surviving spouse liquidates the 401(k) with penalties, sells the house while grieving, and watches everything you built disappear overnight.

Protection planning is tricky because you might never need it. But when you do, it's everything. →

Who Protection Is Really For

One of my most creative clients was an actor-turned-author. He got a later start in life, was older than his wife, and they had one child together. He was adamant about life insurance. We put a solid plan in place to protect his family if the unthinkable ever happened.

And then it did.

One day, his wife called. He'd passed away unexpectedly. Devastating. But because he'd planned ahead, she was able to receive the proceeds tax-free, pay off debt, start saving for retirement, and fund their child's college future. She still calls that policy their family's savior.

This is exactly why protection matters, because when you don't prioritize it, the people you love most are the ones left carrying the burden. →

A 5-Step System for Protection Planning

Here's a practical approach to protection, whether you end up buying insurance or self-insuring:

Step 1: Assess Your Current Situation

Evaluate your income, debts, assets, and family responsibilities. Who depends on you financially?

Step 2: Identify Potential Risks Consider

health issues, disability, death, property damage, and liability. Which ones would devastate your family financially?

Step 3: Understand Different Types of Insurance

Review all options, understanding the pros and cons for your financial goals. Term life is simple and cheap. Disability replaces income. Umbrella policies protect assets. →

Step 4: Calculate Coverage Amounts

Use the Needs-Based Approach (what your family needs) or Human Life Value approach (your earning potential). Don't just guess.

Step 5: Review Regularly

As your life changes, your insurance should too. New baby? More coverage. Kids through college? Maybe less. The bottom line is protection ensures your bridge survives the unexpected.

The Tax Control Triangle (Or Why Most People Pay Too Much in Retirement)

TAX CONTROL **TRIANGLE**

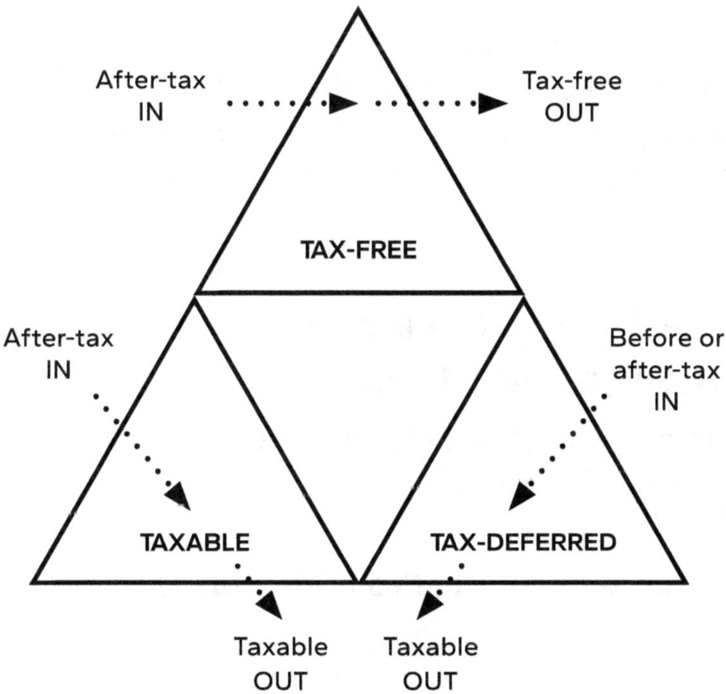

Once you retire, the game completely changes. You're no longer trying to accumulate. You're trying to withdraw without getting killed on taxes.

This is where the **Tax Control Triangle** becomes your secret weapon. By spreading your money across three different tax treatments, you become the CEO of your own tax bill.

Most people miss this. They understand the idea of asset diversification, but they completely overlook tax diversification. And it costs them thousands.

Tax diversification means strategically saving into three buckets, each with different tax consequences. Once you understand why this matters, everything about retirement planning clicks into place.

The Three Buckets That Change Everything

Let me break down the three buckets that make up your Tax Control Triangle:

Taxable Accounts (Your Flexible Money)

This is your regular investment account. You've already paid taxes on this money. You can grab it whenever you want, no age restrictions, no penalties. You only pay capital gains when you sell, which is usually way less than income tax. The downside? You're getting taxed everywhere...when you earn it, every year on dividends, and when you sell.

Think: Brokerage accounts, savings, CDs, that rental property you bought.

Tax-Deferred Accounts (Your Tax-Break Today Money)

Your employer-sponsored retirement plans like the traditional IRA or the 401(k) plan. The government gives you a tax break today, but they're coming for their cut later. Every single dollar you pull out gets taxed as regular income. Great for lowering your taxes now when you're earning big. Not so great when you're retired, and that withdrawal pushes you into a higher bracket.

Think: Traditional 401(k), Traditional IRA, 403(b), pension plans.

Tax-Free Accounts (Your Tax-Free Forever Money)

Your Roth accounts where you pay taxes today, but then it's yours forever, tax-free. Pull out $100,000? You get $100,000. No tax games, no surprises. The catch? No tax deduction today. But honestly, this is the money that lets you sleep at night

Think: Roth IRA, Roth 401(k), Roth conversions, 529 education plans, municipal bonds.

Taxable: Mutual funds, stocks, bonds, checking and savings accounts[1].

Tax-free: Roth IRA[2,3], Roth 401 (k)[2,3], 529 plan[4].

Tax-deferred: 401 (k)[2,5], traditional IRA[2], pension plans[2].

1. Not investments. Interest is taxed as ordinary income.
2. Withdrawal before age fifty-nine-and-a-half may result in a 10 percent IRS penalty on taxable earnings.
3. Necessary requirements must be met. Consult with your tax advisor.
4. When used for qualified higher education expenses; otherwise, you may have to pay income tax plus a 10 percent penalty to the extent of earnings.
5. Special rules apply to appreciated employer securities in qualified retirement plans.

A Roth IRA is tax free as long as investors leave the money in the account for at least five years and are fifty-nine-and-a-half or older when they take distributions or meet another qualifying event.

The 30/40/30 Sweet Spot

After learning about tax diversification, the next question is usually, 'How much should I have in each bucket?"

Unless you know exactly what future tax rates will be, it's impossible to predict. But we've developed a 30/40/30 philosophy that works.

Aim for roughly 30 percent in taxable, 40 percent in tax-deferred, and 30 percent in tax-free. This gives you a great mix, so you can optimize your savings and retirement assets in any tax environment.

Why This Matters (A Real Example)

Let's say you're sixty-seven, retired, and need $80,000 this year. If it all comes from your 401(k), you're pushed into a higher tax bracket, your Medicare premiums spike, and you owe thousands more than necessary.

But if you use the Triangle? You might pull $30,000 from your 401(k), $30,000 from your Roth, and $20,000 from your brokerage account. Same $80,000, way less tax.

Market down? Use your Roth and let the rest recover. Low-income year? Great time for a Roth conversion. Want to avoid the Medicare surcharge threshold? You've got options.

The Tax Control Triangle helps you decide how your money is taxed. In retirement, control is everything. But to make this strategy work, you need to know where to stash your money in the first place.

Where to Save: Beyond the Basics

Your standard 401(k) and IRA are great starting points, but they're just the beginning. There are some serious power moves most people never learn that can optimize your retirement savings.

Here's where to save when you're ready to go beyond the basics:

The Triple Crown Winner: HSAs

If you have a high-deductible health plan, listen up. HSAs are the only account that gives you a tax deduction going in, tax-free growth, *and* tax-free withdrawals for medical expenses. It's the holy grail of tax advantages. Max this out before almost anything else. You can invest it, let it grow for decades, and use it tax-free for medical expenses in retirement. It's a secret retirement account disguised as a health account.[7]

For High Earners Who Got Blocked: Backdoor Strategies

Making too much for a regular Roth IRA? There's still a way in. It's called a backdoor Roth conversion, and it's completely legal. Same goes for mega-backdoor Roth if your 401(k) plan allows after-tax contributions. You can potentially get tens of thousands more into Roth accounts every year.

---

7 Tax laws are subject to change. Consult a tax professional.

For the Self-Employed: Your Own Personal Pension

If you're self-employed or have a side hustle, you've got options regular employees dream about. Solo 401(k)s and SEP IRAs let you save way more than regular accounts. We're talking potentially $60,000 or more per year in tax-advantaged savings.

For Your Kids: 529 Plans

Want to pay for college without getting destroyed by taxes? 529 plans let your money grow tax-free and come out tax-free for education. Some states even give you a tax deduction for contributions. It's like a Roth IRA for college.

The specifics depend on your situation - your income, your employer's plan, your timeline. The principle never changes: use every tax-advantaged account available, in the right order. Start with the free money (employer match), then the triple-tax advantage (HSA), then max out everything else you can.

I know that's a lot to take in. HSAs, backdoor Roths, Solo 401(k)s - it can feel like you need a PhD in tax code. But you don't need to use every strategy I mentioned. You just need to start with one.

So let's talk about how to do that.

Your Next Move: Start Where You Are

The attorney who went from 50 percent to 90 percent retirement probability didn't do anything dramatic. No lottery winnings, no massive raises. Just small, consistent changes that compounded over time.

That's the secret nobody wants to hear because it's boring. But boring works.

Time in the market beats timing the market, every single time. Whether you start with 5 percent or 10 percent, whether you max out everything or just grab the employer match, starting is what matters.

Whether you plan for it or not, you're going to stop working someday. The only question is whether you'll stop because you want to or because you have to.

Nobody gets to the end wishing they'd saved less, planned less, or protected less. So let's build that bridge. Not tomorrow, not next year when things calm down, but now, while you've got time to fortify it.

The people who build the strongest financial bridges aren't just thinking about themselves. They're thinking about what they're building for the people and causes they love. Because once your bridge is solid, we have to start asking new questions.

The ultimate test of a bridge isn't just whether it gets you across; it's whether it's strong enough for the next generation to cross, too.

CHAPTER 6

Your Bridge's Legacy: Estate Planning and Family Impact

YOU'VE BUILT YOUR FINANCIAL bridge. You've got your vision, your plan, and you're making steady progress toward your goals. But what happens to everything you've built if you're not here to manage it?

Welcome to the conversation no one wants to have. Most people squirm when this topic comes up. They'll tackle complex investments, dive into insurance policies, and even face tough debt conversations. But mention estate planning? Suddenly they need to check their phone or grab coffee.

I get it. Estate planning challenges you to think about things you'd rather not. It's uncomfortable.

It's morbid. And it usually involves places I'd rather avoid entirely...the hospital.

I've always hated hospitals. The smell, the food, the heaviness of it all. Someone's sick, someone's dying, or you're waiting for news that's probably not great.

Estate planning feels like that for most people. You don't want to think about being in a coma or worse. The first time I helped my parents create their estate plan, my mom cried through most of it. Not because of the money but because it made everything real.

What I've learned is there's nothing more generous you can do for your family than make a plan. A good estate plan removes all the gray areas. No guessing. No arguments. Just clarity.

Why It Matters More Than You Think

Just like your protection plan, an estate plan isn't for you. It's for the people you love. And it's not just who gets what. It makes sure your family doesn't fall apart when you're no longer here to hold things together.

A clear plan means no one's left wondering what your wishes were. No arguments between siblings about the lake house. Your legacy goes exactly where you want it to with the least amount of stress, taxes, or court involvement.

And yet, most people wait too long. Or never do it at all. That's when things get messy.

This is the biggest risk-to-reward disparity in all of financial planning. The risk of not having an estate plan is huge, especially in blended families with remarriages or children from previous relationships. Without clear instructions, what happens next is left to interpretation.

The One Who Got It Right

Picture a bachelor in his forties — a successful real estate appraiser, fully enjoying the single life. A solid guy who loved life. What surprises most people is how prepared his estate plan was, especially since he had no wife or kids.

At first, I wondered why someone without the "Big Three" would even need a plan. But I came to learn he was continuing a lesson from his own parents.

They had been involved with the Red Cross, and when he was young, he volunteered with them during the 1984 Olympics. That experience stuck with him, and he decided to make the Red Cross his primary beneficiary.

An only child with no surviving family, he didn't need to protect relatives. So, he chose to put his money to work in a meaningful way.

Two years later, he passed away unexpectedly. It was heartbreaking. We had talked over the years about his dream to retire, buy a little place, and travel the world. He never got the chance.

But what he left behind was powerful. I got a call from the Red Cross thanking us for the distributions they received and all the good they could do because of him. I hung up feeling proud and motivated to help more clients leave that kind of legacy.

That's what a good estate plan can do. It turns your intentions into action and creates impact long after you're gone.

The One That Went Completely Sideways

I also watched four siblings tear their family apart over their father's estate. He was wealthy and owned a beautiful California ranch. But after he passed, three siblings stopped speaking to each other.

He had never talked to them about his wishes. Nothing was in writing about some money he'd given one daughter over the years. Now the others wanted it deducted from her share. She said it was a gift. They said it was an advance. Dad wasn't there to explain, and lawyers had to get involved.

All of this could've been avoided with one uncomfortable conversation while he was alive. Just one. Now? Lawyers are getting rich, siblings hate each other, and grandkids lost their cousins.

Don't let the first time your kids hear your wishes be when the attorney reads them aloud.

Legacy Is More Than Money

Money can make people act irrationally. When someone with wealth doesn't talk to their family, it creates a ticking time bomb. Silent expectations and lack of transparency can tear a family apart, and I doubt that's the legacy you want.

Part of a complete plan is not just creating the documents but talking to your *fam*ily about them.

Creating the trust itself requires an estate planning attorney. But getting it done and having those crucial conversations with family is the goal. When families communicate openly about money and values, they avoid conflicts that can tear families apart after a loved one passes.

Estate planning can change a family tree for the better.

I've seen clients carve out $50,000 for a struggling nephew. Set up college funds that send three generations to school. Pay off student loans unexpectedly.

That's life-changing.

Estate planning is how your bridge goes far beyond just money. It becomes legacy.

Estate Planning: The Final Step in Your Legacy

Here are the steps to put in place:

Meet with an estate planning attorney (or use a reputable online service). Pay the small fee; it's surprisingly affordable for the stability you'll gain.

Put these five documents in place:

Revocable Living Trust - avoids probate and ensures smooth asset transfer.

Pour-Over Will - ensures assets outside the trust are still covered.

Durable Power of Attorney - lets someone manage finances if you're incapacitated.

Advance Health Care Directive - outlines your medical wishes.

Guardianship Designations - critical if you have minor children.

You don't need it all figured out. Just take the first step. You can always revise later, but having *something* is far better than leaving your family with uncertainty.

An estate plan prevents confusion, avoids conflict,

and protects the people you love most.

Your legacy isn't just what you leave behind; it's the care you put into planning for it. Your estate plan is the final piece of the bridge you've worked so hard to build.

Start Now, Start Small, Just Start

I know this feels heavy. But the risk of not doing this is high, *especially* for blended families, and the bar to start is so low. There's no excuse.

Start now. Start small. Just start.

You'll sleep better knowing your family will be taken care of exactly as you intended.

But even the best estate plan can't protect you from every challenge. Markets crash. Jobs disappear. Parents get sick. Kids need help.

Your bridge must withstand storms. We're talking about how to keep your bridge strong when life gets real next.

CHAPTER 7

When Life Happens – Staying Strong Through Every Season

ANYONE CAN FEEL LIKE a financial genius when everything's clicking. Markets are up, job's solid, life's running on autopilot. But bridges aren't built for perfect weather. If your plan only works when life's easy, that's not a plan. It's a wish.

Life throws curveballs. That's the only guarantee. And when storms hit, when the unexpected disrupts your income, your family, or your future, the question is if your bridge can handle it.

After two decades in financial planning, the patterns are consistent. Marriages, divorces, layoffs, market crashes, parents moving in, and adult children needing support.

The families who weathered those storms and came out stronger weren't lucky. They were prepared. They had built something designed to flex, to bend, to hold.

Because life doesn't unfold in a straight line. Neither should your financial plan. Yet every financial tool out there assumes it does.

The Fantasy of Linear Planning

Simple retirement calculators feel great. Enter your income, your target age, your expected return, and, boom, you're set. Save this much for twenty-five years with no interruptions, and you're golden.

That's not how life works.

I've sat with hundreds of families who learned this the hard way. They had the spreadsheets, the calculators, the projections. What they didn't have was a plan that could handle reality.

People in their forties and fifties are juggling everything. They are paying for travel soccer while researching Medicare supplements, weddings, aging parents, and unexpected health issues...all at once.

I see the exhaustion when they're calculating college tuition while Googling assisted living costs. They always ask the same thing. "Am I doing enough?"

That's why real planning matters, just like it mattered for the Golden Gate Bridge. It didn't rise out of the bay on schedule. There were massive setbacks. Political, structural, and economic. The plan got challenged, revised, and reworked. But they never abandoned the vision. They adapted, adjusted, and stayed disciplined. And eventually, they created one of the most iconic bridges in history.

That's what it takes to build something worth crossing.

So let's get real about what happens when your perfectly planned bridge meets real life. The first challenges are the milestones you've been looking forward to.

Marriage, Mortgages, and Kids: The Big Three

Life's biggest celebrations have a way of shaking everything up. I call them the Big Three because they reshape your life.

Marriage. Mortgages. Children.

I'm not speaking theoretically. I've been married for over a decade, have three kids, and multiple mortgages.

Building a plan while living through the same milestones makes the advice real.. You can't fake knowing what it feels like when your water heater breaks the same week your kid needs braces, and the property tax bill arrives.

Back when I was younger, I could run perfect mortgage numbers for clients. After buying my first house, I learned how messy it gets. Spreadsheets don't show the lender losing your documents, the 2 a.m. panic when the appraisal comes in low, or the quiet relief when you finally get the keys.

Anyone who has been through this stage knows both the math and the reality. I know where people stumble and what they'll thank themselves for doing early. The Big Three become the first real weight your bridge has to carry.

Handle them right, and you'll stabilize. Build in enough flexibility, and you'll be ready for what comes next. Because just when you've got the rhythm down of mortgage payments flowing, kids thriving, and careers humming, your parents start needing help.

Caught in the Middle: Pressure from Both Sides

Welcome to the sandwich generation where the pressure doubles.

You're writing summer camp checks while helping your parents downsize from the house they've had for forty years. You're setting up 529s while touring senior communities.

Think about someone who watched their parents lose everything — forced to sell their home, ending up with very little. Decades of hard work, and they're choosing between groceries and medications in retirement.

A plan was put in place to help her parents downsize into something manageable. For a couple years, it worked. Her parents settled into a smaller place, and her kids saw them often. Then her dad's health declined.

After he passed, we pivoted again. Her mom moved into the guest house, which became a gift to everyone. Grandma got more time with her grandkids, and Mom got help with childcare while at work.

A complete 180 from crisis to solution. Challenging? Absolutely. But it was only doable because she had built her bridge strong enough to carry extra weight. Her parents' setbacks could have pulled everyone down. Instead, she had the margin to help without sacrificing her own family's future.

That's what real planning does. It protects your bridge and, more importantly, the people counting on it.

When to Tweak vs. When to Pivot

Today, tomorrow and in the future...

Be prepared...

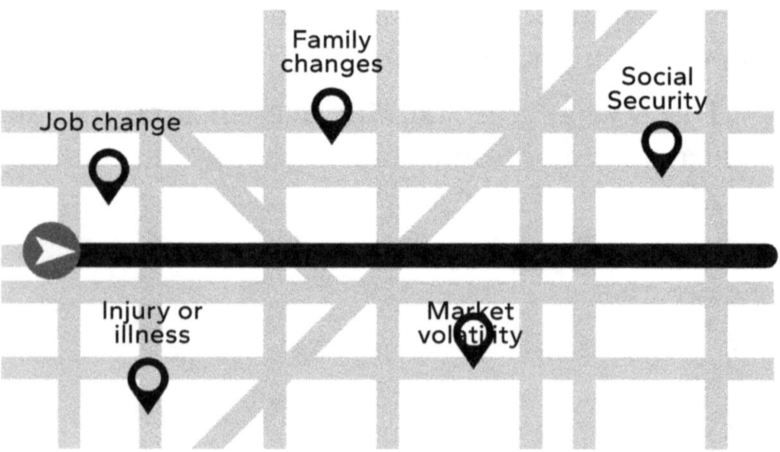

When things go sideways, most people panic. They assume their whole plan is shot. But usually the plan doesn't need to be scrapped. It just needs adjusted.

I've learned that, if the math works but your spending doesn't, that's an adjustment. If the math itself doesn't work anymore, that's when you need to pivot.

A couple helped their daughter with a home down payment and worried they'd wrecked their retirement. When we ran the numbers, all they needed was to skip a couple of vacations and delay the kitchen remodel. That's an *adjustment*. A few behavioral changes were all it took.

In retirement, people sometimes go off script. They help their kids, take extra trips, and spend more than planned. Most times, these are blips. The bridge is solid; it just needs a tune-up.

When the damage runs deeper, you have a structural problem. When spending has outpaced income or a medical emergency creates massive bills, rising costs require more than behavioral tweaks. That's when we consider bigger changes, like downsizing, delaying retirement, or going back to work.

Those conversations aren't easy, but they're necessary. A sound financial plan acts like an engineer for your bridge. The numbers tell you when something is off track and what adjustments will course correct.

Sometimes the storm isn't just hitting your house; it's hitting everyone's. Market crashes, pandemics, and recessions are when having steady hands on your financial bridge matters most.

What Two Crashes Taught Me About Staying the Course

The 2008 Financial Crisis and the Covid Crash of 2020 both created panic. Both tested every plan we'd built. The outcomes were different though. In 2008, the market dropped and stayed down for years. In 2020, it fell fast and rebounded almost as quickly.

What was identical? The fear in people's voices. The phones were ringing nonstop with panicked questions. People watching accounts drop 40 percent, wondering if everything they'd worked for was vanishing. The work in those moments wasn't just managing money; it was managing emotions and staying grounded when every instinct screamed to run.

I reminded clients that this wasn't new. History says staying invested works. But knowing that when your retirement's tanking? Entirely different. The difference between the clients who survived and those who thrived wasn't their portfolio. It was their ability to sit tight when everything in them wanted to run.

By 2020, I had my own skin in the game, but the playbook was the same. Show up, stay calm, and take the calls. Every email, every conversation was a chance to be the steady voice in the storm.

The clients who stuck with the plan through both crashes are bulletproof now. Markets wobble, and they shrug. They've seen their bridge hold through hurricane-force winds.

Those two crashes taught me you can't control markets or fear. You control whether you show up. Whether you stay consistent. Whether you have the guts to stay boring when everyone else is panicking. That's what gets people through.

Build to Bend, Not Break

No plan is perfect. Every bridge creaks when winds pick up. That's not cause for alarm. It's your plan working as intended, absorbing stress, flexing where needed, holding steady.

I've walked this path with clients through every storm imaginable. Seen bridges sway, watched them bend, celebrated when they held. The secret isn't genius or timing. It's being ready for anything, staying flexible when plans blow up, and having a plan that accounts for the terrain..

You might be thinking, "You might be thinking, *'Easy to say when you've been studying this for years.'*" Fair. But every client started where you are, worried, uncertain, and wondering if it's enough. They didn't have all the answers. They just started anyway.

You're going to make mistakes. You'll help your kids when you probably shouldn't. You'll panic-sell something in a downturn. You'll buy the boat. We all do it. The goal is having a plan strong enough to handle your human moments. Strong enough that when you mess up (and you will), the whole thing doesn't collapse.

You don't need a flawless plan. You need a resilient one. Storms will come. But panic? That's optional.

Your plan won't be perfect. Mine isn't either. But when life throws its next curveball, you'll be ready. You built something that can take the hit. That's all any of us are really doing here. We're building bridges strong enough to carry the people we love through whatever comes next.

True wealth isn't just money. It's relationships, health, and purpose. That's where we're headed next.

CHAPTER 8

Beyond Money - Building Success in Every Area

MONEY AND WEALTH ARE not the same thing. It took me years to figure that out.

Money matters, of course. But there comes a point where your definition of success starts to shift. The bank account might be growing, the business might be thriving, but something still feels off. That's when you realize real wealth isn't just about numbers on a statement. It's about health, relationships, energy, and purpose. All the stuff that doesn't show up on a balance sheet but absolutely shows up in your life.

I didn't always believe that. In fact, there was a stretch where I was living the exact opposite, and it nearly cost me everything we'd worked for.

The Year We Stopped Growing

Ten years in, my business partner and I became very negative about everything. We had been working really hard for a decade, and all of a sudden, our attitude shifted from humble and hard-working to entitlement. We thought we were owed more support, more resources, more pay.

We'd spend hours complaining about resources from the firm, convincing ourselves everyone else had it better. The company didn't support us, the whole system was rigged against us. Classic victim mentality, but we couldn't see it.

The tough thing about sharing a negative mindset with your business partner is that misery loves company. We would just complain together, and we thought this is the way it was. We convinced ourselves we were telling the truth about our situation. No resources, business is hard, the grass is greener somewhere else.

In our twenty-year partnership, that year of negativity and complaining was the only year that our business did not grow.

We were the problem.

The wake-up call came at a company-wide conference. Everyone gathered, results were shared, and it was usually a celebration. But that year? While our friends and colleagues had milestone numbers, ours came in at the lowest.

Everyone else was having their best year ever. Same company, same resources, same challenges, but they were talking about opportunities while we were drowning in our own complaints. Hard to keep blaming the system when everyone in the system is winning except you.

Our negative attitude wasn't a response to our situation. It was creating our situation.

That realization hit hard. When you've been grinding for ten years and suddenly see that your attitude is the roadblock, it forces you to look for solutions in new places. Where your focus goes, energy flows. We'd been focusing on problems, so that's all we got. Time to focus on something better.

The GOAT Decade: Why Mindset Shapes Results

My sister happened to be getting into personal development and recommended a podcast. I wasn't exactly the self-help type. But after seeing our business flatline while our colleagues thrived, I figured I'd check it out. I never wanted to repeat that year of zero growth again.

It changed everything.

The biggest shift was learning that what you focus on grows, and we'd been focusing on all the wrong things. I became obsessed with this stuff, and my enthusiasm eventually intrigued my business partner. After being negative for so long, we were both ready for change.

We went all in. Most people consume self-help like gym memberships. Buy in January, forget by February. We applied it and have been ever since. Morning workouts. Gratitude journals. Writing down goals and reviewing them regularly. Research consistently shows that people who write down their goals and share them with others are far more likely to follow through.

I know how this sounds. If you'd told me I'd be the guy with a gratitude journal, I would've laughed. But when you realize you're going to blink and five years will disappear anyway, you might as well make them good years.

The more we focused on where we wanted to go instead of what was wrong, the clearer everything became. We finally understood why we were grinding so hard. And it wasn't just to keep up with the LA lifestyle.

That was the beginning of what we now call our **GOAT Decade.** Growth, Opportunity, Abundance, Thriving. We came up with the name at the end of 2019, looking back at everything we'd been through the previous decade. The wins, the burnout, the mindset traps, and asked ourselves, "What could life look like ten years from now if we did it differently?"

That became our filter. Hit a setback? We'd ask, "Is this mindset helping us grow? Are we looking for opportunity?" If not, we course-corrected.

The GOAT Decade wasn't just a motto. It was a commitment. A decision to spend the next ten years building a business and life around possibility instead of negativity.

That shift didn't just change how we ran the business. It changed how I showed up everywhere. You can't compartmentalize success. The same habits that poison your work poison everything else.

How You Do One Thing is How You Do Everything

How you handle the small stuff reveals everything about how you'll handle the big stuff. If you're sloppy with your workout routine, you'll be sloppy with your budget, too. Running late to meetings turns into running behind on financial goals. It's all connected. Your money habits, your health habits, your relationship habits. Once you see the pattern, you can't unsee it.

Embracing this mindset is liberating. It means you don't need some massive personality overhaul to get your finances right. You just need to start being intentional about the small stuff.

People tend to think they can excel in one area while coasting in others. Doesn't work that way.

A friend of mine was living proof of this. Top sales performer, always energized, everyone loved him. He'd show up to every company event. The Lakers games, client dinners, and conferences, giving his all.

I assumed he brought that same energy home.

But no. He'd close $1 million deals then forget his daughter's recital. He was a hero at work but completely absent at his own dinner table. His kids stopped asking if Dad would make it to their practices. His wife was essentially a single parent with a husband who visited occasionally.

He was Superman at work. Clark Kent at home.

Watching him struggle made me examine my own priorities. Your kids won't remember your biggest deal. They'll remember whether you showed up. Your spouse won't care about your promotion if you're never present.

Real wealth means being intentional about where you spend your energy. Work matters. Financial goals matter. But when you're so focused on making money that you're missing life, you're doing it backwards.

And if you stop there, you miss the bigger picture of

what matters most.

What Are You Really Building?

I still have days when the old negativity creeps in, when I don't show up the way I want. The difference now is that I catch myself faster. Progress beats perfection every time.

It wasn't always like that. There was a time when success seemed to mean having enough money that nothing could touch you. That thinking changes. Real success is being able to look at your health, your relationships, your purpose, your money and honestly say you're showing up for all of it.

You can build the most impressive financial bridge in the world. But if you're too burned out to cross it, too unhealthy to make the journey, or have nobody to share the view with, what's the point?

The strongest bridges aren't just steel and concrete. They're built by people who live with purpose, not just chase success. At some point, you stop building just for yourself. You start thinking about what you're leaving behind. Not just the money but the impact, the lessons, the legacy.

Let's talk about what that really means.

CONCLUSION

No Regrets – Start Building Today

IF YOU'VE MADE IT this far, something in this book connected with you. That means you're ready to stop dreaming and start laying down the foundation for the life you want.

Let me take you back to the Golden Gate Bridge.

When it was first imagined, most said it couldn't be done. The strait was too deep. The winds, too fierce. But one man, Joseph Strauss, had a vision. He believed it was possible. And with that vision and a plan to match, he made it happen. His mantra was simple. "It *can* be done."

When the bridge finally opened in 1937, it wasn't just the longest suspension bridge in the world. Built during the Great Depression, it became a symbol of hope. It was proof that with enough persistence, courage, and belief, even the impossible could be built.

That bridge still stands today. Yours can, too, standing strong for generations. But only if you stop planning and start doing. The ones who build something? Action, pure and simple.

Stop Talking, Start Building

The reality is that nothing happens without action. You need a vision; that's the other side of your bridge. You need a plan; that's where you begin. Most of all, you need consistency, discipline, and the grit to keep going when it gets hard.

The blueprint is here. Now comes the hard part. Doing it.

Vision comes first. What does success look like? Until you define it, you're just wandering with a hammer, looking for nails.

Once you see it, it's time to put in the reps. The people who win in the long run are the ones who stay consistent. They show up. They save when it's hard. They get back on track when life knocks them sideways. And they keep going.

That's how real bridges get built. One beam at a time. One day at a time.

"I Wish I'd Started Sooner..."

If you're thinking, *"Why didn't I do this ten years ago?"*, welcome to the club. That feeling is universal.

Beating yourself up doesn't build anything. You're here now. That's what matters. Many people feel that regret and then shut down. They hide. They do nothing. You didn't do that. You showed up. You're reading this. You're ready to move.

The courage it takes to say, "Okay, time to get serious," that's something to be proud of. Starting today is always better than starting tomorrow. Because if you keep showing up for the next ten, fifteen, or thirty years, you'll be amazed by what's possible.

You're going to mess up. Miss a savings goal. Overspend. That's being human. The difference between success and failure isn't perfection; it's getting back on track faster each time you drift. And when you do that long enough, something interesting happens.

The Bridge Made of Steel

Think about a steel bridge. Over time, it gets stronger. Sure, you've got to fix some rust or tighten a bolt, but the structure holds. It stands the test of time.

That's what a good financial plan should do. Handle whatever life throws at you. After decades of discipline, saving, and small adjustments, your financial bridge becomes something you and your family can count on.

And that's the real goal. Making sure it holds long after you're gone. The best example I can give you comes from two teachers I worked with.

The Couple Who Proved It's Never Too Late

He was a junior high teacher. She was a vice principal. Salt-of-the-earth people in their mid-fifties. They raised their kids in the same home in Redondo Beach and spent their lives pouring into others by volunteering, coaching, and serving their community. These were the types of people everyone gravitated toward.

They had solid pensions but not much savings. For years, it was all about their kids and careers. When we sat down, they were ready to make a change.

They wanted to retire in that same home and stay connected to the community they loved. But costs were rising fast. We ran the numbers. They had to make a choice to give up the dream or make some serious adjustments.

They chose the dream. Aligned and ready, they committed to saving 20 percent of their income for the next ten years. No fancy tricks. No get-rich schemes. Just disciplined saving.

And they did it.

They pushed through. Stayed focused. When they retired, their bridge was built. Maybe they didn't start early, but they finished strong. Now they're living their vision, still in their home by the beach, beloved by their community, loving every minute.

They're proof it's never about perfection. It's about staying the course. And once you've done that, once you've built something solid, you start thinking differently about what it all means.

What Will They Say About You?

Let's get heavy for a minute. Imagine your funeral.

I know. But stick with me.

Who's there? What do they say?

Nobody talks about your 401(k) or Q3 projections. They talk about the kind of person you were. How you showed up. Who you loved. What kind of parent, spouse, or friend you were.

Legacy isn't about numbers. It's about impact.

Money is just a tool that amplifies what you already are. If your values are about memories, love, and showing up, your plan should help you do more of that. The stronger your bridge, the more people can walk across it with you.

That exercise puts everything in perspective. Now let's channel that clarity into action.

You Can Do This

This journey isn't easy. But if you're reading this, you can build a financial bridge that lasts.

It takes grit. Sacrifice. Focus. Time.

You won't build it overnight. But if you keep showing up, keep laying down steel, one decision at a time, it gets done. Get rich slow. It's the only way that works. The flashy stuff? Bridges made of straw. One strong wind, they're gone.

Ready to build something that actually holds?

Here's Exactly What You Do Next

No more theory. Just three steps.

Step 1: Envision your bridge. Go somewhere quiet. Bring your spouse if you have one. Write down what you want your money to accomplish. Not vague goals. Be specific. What does a regular Tuesday look like in your dream life?

Step 2: Take action today. Not next week. Today. Bump up your 401(k). Set up a savings transfer. Call HR. Do one thing that moves you forward.

Step 3: Stay disciplined. This isn't a sprint. It's showing up every day for years. That's what builds the bridge. That's what makes it strong.

One Last Look at the Bridge

→ The Golden Gate (2024)

An engineering marvel designed to bend without breaking. The Golden Gate's massive 746-foot towers hold up two main cables containing enough wire to wrap around the Earth three times. Built to withstand brutal winds and currents, the bridge can safely sway up to twenty-seven feet sideways to absorb the storm. Its span is a living testament to connection. Standing 746 feet above the Pacific, the Golden Gate Bridge carries over 112,000 people every single day and has safely transported more than 2 billion travelers since 1937.

The Golden Gate Bridge still stands because someone had vision, took action, and stuck with it even when it was hard.

That's exactly what your bridge needs, too.

You've read this far. That tells me you're ready. Ready to stop hoping and start building. Ready to create something that lasts for you and for the people you love.

Here's the final challenge. Picture your bridge. Decide where it leads. Then start building. Today.

Will it be easy? No. Will you want to quit? Probably. But can you do it? Absolutely. It takes work, sacrifice, grit, and consistency. But it's possible.

The blueprint is here. You've got what you need. Now pick up the tools.

One day at a time. One decision at a time.

That's how bridges get built. That's how lives get changed.

Let's get to work. Your future self is counting on it.

→ *From left to right: Nick, Kristin, Cailey, and Travis.* We took a trip to Napa Valley.

ABOUT THE AUTHORS

Travis Gabler, MS, CFP®, BFA™, CRPC™, AAMS®, CMFC™, AWMA®, MPAS™

Travis Gabler has spent more than two decades in the financial services industry, earning one of the most extensive credential portfolios in the profession. He holds a Master of Science in Personal Financial Planning from the College for Financial Planning and a Bachelor of Business Administration from Loyola Marymount University.

His work has been recognized by Forbes on multiple occasions, including listings for Best-in-State Wealth Advisors, Best-in-State Next-Generation Wealth Advisors, and Top Next-Generation Wealth Advisors. He has also received the Five Star Wealth Manager designation for more than a dozen consecutive years.

Travis has been a donor and active participant with the Boys and Girls Club for more than fifteen years and remains a committed supporter and alumnus of Loyola Marymount University. He lives in Los Angeles with his wife, Cailey, and their three children, Elyse, Lucas, and Grayson.

Nicholas Nino, CFP®

Nicholas Nino brings nineteen years of financial services experience to this book, with a background built on years of study in personal finance, retirement strategy, and tax planning. He holds a Bachelor of Arts in History from Loyola Marymount University and earned his CERTIFIED FINANCIAL PLANNER® designation through years of professional study and practice

Nick has been named to Forbes Best-in-State Wealth Advisors and Forbes Top Next-Generation Wealth Advisors, and was recognized by Financial Planning magazine as a Top 40 Regional Advisor Under 40. He has also received the Five Star Wealth Manager designation across multiple years.

Outside of work, Nick is a youth sports coach, an active community volunteer, and a passionate advocate for financial literacy. He lives in the Westlake Village area with his family.

www.ingramcontent.com/pod-product-compliance
Lightning Source LLC
LaVergne TN
LVHW022008200926
848481LV00007B/2291
* 9 7 9 8 9 5 0 5 8 3 0 1 8 *

www.ingramcontent.com/pod-product-compliance
Lightning Source LLC
LaVergne TN
LVHW022006200926
848481LV00007B/2253